Wisdom and Revelation

Wisdom and Revelation

Compiled by Eugene Carvalho

To the Body of Christ.
May this compilation bless you richly!
With love…

TABLE OF CONTENTS

PURPOSE AND ACKNOWLEDGEMENTS

The infallible Word of God for faith and conduct informs us that the Holy Spirit gives gifts to men and women of the Body of Christ. It states: "the gifts edify the body for the building up of the saints" (Eph. 4:12). I hope the talents and gifts the Lord has given me will be a blessing to someone else through the reading of this compilation.

I am grateful for the love and support from my wonderful wife Mercedes. I am also grateful for the knowledge, wisdom and love of many pastors, teachers, and saints that the Lord has used to bless me.

WISDOM AND REVELATION

I have heard over the years that the book of Ephesians is the warfare book in the New Testament. However, Ephesians and Colossians are twin epistles. "There is a striking similarity between Ephesians and Colossians. Seventy-eight out of 155 verses are identical or nearly identical."[1] Therefore, I personally engage myself in the study of these two aforementioned books at great lengths.

The Apostle Paul, one of the greatest minds western civilization has ever seen, wrote, "For this reason I too, having heard of the faith in the Lord Jesus which exists among you and your love for all the saints, do not cease giving thanks for you, while making mention of you in my prayers; that the God of our Lord Jesus Christ, the Father of glory, may give to you a spirit of wisdom and of revelation in the knowledge of Him" (Eph. 1:15-17).[2]

In these end times, whoever has revelation knowledge will rule the earth. God's people must rise up and live and operate the way Jesus did while He was on earth. Jesus came to show us the potential that we have inside of us. "A mere knowledge of God's Word is not what will please Him. We need to be controlled by that knowledge.

---

[1] James E. Smith, *The New Testament Books Made Simple*, (College Press, 2009), p. 85.

[2] All Scripture quotations, unless otherwise noted, are from the *New American Standard Bible*.

The word fill means to control. To be filled with something (an emotion like fear or jealousy) means to be under its controlling influence that causes us to do things we might not do otherwise. Being controlled by God's will should cause us to do things we might not otherwise do—things like enduring rather than giving up, like being patient with others rather than getting angry with them.

"The knowledge and control of God's will comes through all spiritual wisdom and understanding. This is more than simple intelligence. Wisdom refers to the comprehension of truth, while understanding refers to the application of truth. Being controlled by God's will means believers comprehend the principles of Scripture and then put them into practice."[3]

If you were to ask me, "brother Gene, what would be the most important thing you could inform me so I can go to new levels?" It would be stewardship regarding your time is what will take you to new levels. For the most part, I believe it all comes down to spending time in the Word and the secret place. The more time you spend in those two locations, the higher and greater the mountain of influence the Lord will trust you with.

With that being said, let's examine a vast array of infallible scriptures that discuss wisdom and revelation.

---

[3] Max Anders, *Galatians-Colossians, vol. 8, Holman New Testament Commentary* (Nashville, TN: Broadman & Holman Publishers, 1999), 281.

WISDOM IN THE OLD TESTAMENT

WISDOM IN THE BOOK OF EXODUS

Endowed with the Spirit of Wisdom

"Then bring near to yourself Aaron your brother, and his sons with him, from among the sons of Israel, to minister as priest to Me — Aaron, Nadab and Abihu, Eleazar and Ithamar, Aaron's sons. You shall make holy garments for Aaron your brother, for glory and for beauty. You shall speak to all the skillful persons whom I have endowed with the spirit of wisdom, that they make Aaron's garments to consecrate him, that he may minister as priest to Me. These are the garments which they shall make: a breastpiece and an ephod and a robe and a tunic of checkered work, a turban and a sash, and they shall make holy garments for Aaron your brother and his sons, that he may minister as priest to Me. They shall take the gold and the blue and the purple and the scarlet material and the fine linen" (Ex. 28:1-5).

Filled Him with the Spirit of God in Wisdom

"Now the Lord spoke to Moses, saying, 'See, I have called by name Bezalel, the son of Uri, the son of Hur, of the tribe of Judah. I have filled him with the Spirit of God in wisdom, in understanding, in knowledge, and in all kinds of craftsmanship, to make artistic designs for work in gold, in silver, and in bronze, and in the cutting of stones for settings, and in the carving of wood, that he may work in all kinds of craftsmanship. And behold, I Myself have appointed with him Oholiab, the son of Ahisamach, of the tribe of Dan; and in the hearts of all who are skillful I have put skill, that they may make all that I have commanded you: the tent of meeting, and the ark of testimony, and the mercy seat upon it, and all the furniture of the tent, the table also and its utensils, and the pure gold lampstand with all its utensils, and the altar of incense, the altar of burnt offering also with all its utensils, and the laver and its stand, the woven garments as well, and the holy garments for Aaron the priest, and the garments of his sons, with which to carry on their priesthood; the anointing oil also, and the fragrant incense for the holy place, they are to make them according to all that I have commanded you'" (Ex. 31:1-11).

In Wisdom, in Understanding and in Knowledge

"Then Moses said to the sons of Israel, 'See, the Lord has called by name Bezalel the son of Uri, the son of Hur, of the tribe of Judah. And He has filled him with the Spirit of God, in wisdom, in understanding and in knowledge and in all craftsmanship; to make designs for working in gold and in silver and in bronze, and in the cutting of stones for settings and in the carving of wood, so as to perform in every inventive work. He also has put in his heart to teach, both he and Oholiab, the son of Ahisamach, of the tribe of Dan. He has filled them with skill to perform every work of an engraver and of a designer and of an embroiderer, in blue and in purple and in scarlet material, and in fine linen, and of a weaver, as performers of every work and makers of designs" (Ex. 35:30-35).

WISDOM IN THE BOOK OF DEUTERONOMY

That Is Your Wisdom and Your Understanding

"See, I have taught you statutes and judgments just as the Lord God commanded me, that you should do thus in the land where you are entering to possess it. So keep and do them, for that is your wisdom and your understanding in the sight of the peoples who will hear all these statutes and say, 'Surely this great nation is a wise and understanding people.' For what great nation is there that has a god so near to it as is the Lord our God whenever we call on Him? Or what great nation is there that has statutes and judgments as righteous as this whole law which I am setting before you today?" (Dt. 4:5-8).

Was Filled with the Spirit of Wisdom

"Now Joshua the son of Nun was filled with the spirit of wisdom, for Moses had laid his hands on him; and the sons of Israel listened to him and did as the Lord had commanded Moses. Since that time no prophet has risen in Israel like Moses, whom the Lord knew face to face, for all the signs and wonders which the Lord sent him to perform in the land of Egypt against Pharaoh, all his servants, and all his land, and for all the mighty power and for all the great terror which Moses performed in the sight of all Israel" (Dt. 34:9-12).

WISDOM IN THE BOOK OF 2 SAMUEL

Like the Wisdom of the Angel of God

"Then the king answered and said to the woman, 'Please do not hide anything from me that I am about to ask you.' And the woman said, 'Let my lord the king please speak.' So the king said, 'Is the hand of Joab with you in all this?' And the woman replied, 'As your soul lives, my lord the king, no one can turn to the right or to the left from anything that my lord the king has spoken. Indeed, it was your servant Joab who commanded me, and it was he who put all these words in the mouth of your maidservant; in order to change the appearance of things your servant Joab has done this thing. But my lord is wise, like the wisdom of the angel of God, to know all that is in the earth'" (2 Sa. 14:18-20).

WISDOM IN THE BOOK OF 1 KINGS

Act According to your Wisdom

"Now you also know what Joab the son of Zeruiah did to me, what he did to the two commanders of the armies of Israel, to Abner the son of Ner, and to Amasa the son of Jether, whom he killed; he also shed the blood of war in peace. And he put the blood of war on his belt about his waist, and on his sandals on his feet. So act according to your wisdom, and do not let his gray hair go down to Sheol in peace. But show kindness to the sons of Barzillai the Gileadite, and let them be among those who eat at your table; for they assisted me when I fled from Absalom your brother. Behold, there is with you Shimei the son of Gera the Benjamite, of Bahurim; now it was he who cursed me with a violent curse on the day I went to Mahanaim. But when he came down to me at the Jordan, I swore to him by the Lord, saying, 'I will not put you to death with the sword.' Now therefore, do not let him go unpunished, for you are a wise man; and you will know what you ought to do to him, and you will bring his gray hair down to Sheol with blood" (1 Ki. 2:5-9).

The Wisdom of God Was in Him

"Then the king said, 'The one says, "This is my son who is living, and your son is the dead one"; and the other says, "No! For your son is the dead one, and my son is the living one.'" The king said, 'Get me a sword.' So they brought a sword before the king. The king said, 'Divide the living child in two, and give half to the one and half to the other.' Then the woman whose child was the living one spoke to the king, for she was deeply stirred over her son and said, 'Oh, my lord, give her the living child, and by no means kill him.' But the other said, 'He shall be neither mine nor yours; divide him!' Then the king said, 'Give the first woman the living child, and by no means kill him. She is his mother.' When all Israel heard of the judgment which the king had handed down, they feared the king, for they saw that the wisdom of God was in him to administer justice" (1 Ki. 3:23-28).

Wisdom and Very Great Discernment

"Now God gave Solomon wisdom and very great discernment and breadth of mind, like the sand that is on the seashore. Solomon's wisdom surpassed the wisdom of all the sons of the east and all the wisdom of Egypt. For he was wiser than all men, than Ethan the Ezrahite, Heman, Calcol and Darda, the sons of Mahol; and his fame was known in all the surrounding nations. He also spoke 3,000 proverbs, and his songs were 1,005. He spoke of trees, from the cedar that is in Lebanon even to the hyssop that grows on the wall; he spoke also of animals and birds and creeping things and fish. Men came from all peoples to hear the wisdom of Solomon, from all the kings of the earth who had heard of his wisdom" (1 Ki. 4:29-34).

The Lord Gave Wisdom to Solomon

"When Hiram heard the words of Solomon, he rejoiced greatly and said, 'Blessed be the Lord today, who has given to David a wise son over this great people.' So Hiram sent word to Solomon, saying, 'I have heard the message which you have sent me; I will do what you desire concerning the cedar and cypress timber. My servants will bring them down from Lebanon to the sea; and I will make them into rafts to go by sea to the place where you direct me, and I will have them broken up there, and you shall carry them away. Then you shall accomplish my desire by giving food to my household.' So Hiram gave Solomon as much as he desired of the cedar and cypress timber. Solomon then gave Hiram 20,000 kors of wheat as food for his household, and twenty kors of beaten oil; thus Solomon would give Hiram year by year. The Lord gave wisdom to Solomon, just as He promised him; and there was peace between Hiram and Solomon, and the two of them made a covenant" (1 Ki. 5:7-12).

Filled with Wisdom and Understanding and Skill

"Now King Solomon sent and brought Hiram from Tyre. He was a widow's son from the tribe of Naphtali, and his father was a man of Tyre, a worker in bronze; and he was filled with wisdom and understanding and skill for doing any work in bronze. So he came to King Solomon and performed all his work" (1 Ki. 7:13-14).

Perceived All the Wisdom of Solomon

"Now when the queen of Sheba heard about the fame of Solomon concerning the name of the Lord, she came to test him with difficult questions. So she came to Jerusalem with a very large retinue, with camels carrying spices and very much gold and precious stones. When she came to Solomon, she spoke with him about all that was in her heart. Solomon answered all her questions; nothing was hidden from the king which he did not explain to her. When the queen of Sheba perceived all the wisdom of Solomon, the house that he had built, the food of his table, the seating of his servants, the attendance of his waiters and their attire, his cupbearers, and his stairway by which he went up to the house of the Lord, there was no more spirit in her. Then she said to the king, 'It was a true report which I heard in my own land about your words and your wisdom. Nevertheless I did not believe the reports, until I came and my eyes had seen it. And behold, the half was not told me. You exceed in wisdom and prosperity the report which I heard. How blessed are your men, how blessed are these your servants who stand before you continually and hear your wisdom. Blessed be the Lord your God who delighted in you to set you on the throne of Israel; because the Lord loved Israel forever, therefore He made you king, to do justice and righteousness.' She gave the king a hundred and twenty talents of gold, and a very great amount of spices and precious stones. Never again did such abundance of spices come in as that which the queen of Sheba gave King Solomon" (1 Ki. 10:1-10).

In Riches and in Wisdom

"So King Solomon became greater than all the kings of the earth in riches and in wisdom. All the earth was seeking the presence of Solomon, to hear his wisdom which God had put in his heart. They brought every man his gift, articles of silver and gold, garments, weapons, spices, horses, and mules, so much year by year" (1 Ki. 10:23-25).

His Wisdom

"Now the rest of the acts of Solomon and whatever he did, and his wisdom, are they not written in the book of the acts of Solomon? Thus the time that Solomon reigned in Jerusalem over all Israel was forty years. And Solomon slept with his fathers and was buried in the city of his father David, and his son Rehoboam reigned in his place" (1 Ki. 11:41-43).

WISDOM IN THE BOOK OF 2 CHRONICLES

Give Me Now Wisdom and Knowledge

"In that night God appeared to Solomon and said to him, 'Ask what I shall give you.' Solomon said to God, 'You have dealt with my father David with great lovingkindness, and have made me king in his place. Now, O Lord God, Your promise to my father David is fulfilled, for You have made me king over a people as numerous as the dust of the earth. Give me now wisdom and knowledge, that I may go out and come in before this people, for who can rule this great people of Yours?' God said to Solomon, 'Because you had this in mind, and did not ask for riches, wealth or honor, or the life of those who hate you, nor have you even asked for long life, but you have asked for yourself wisdom and knowledge that you may rule My people over whom I have made you king, wisdom and knowledge have been granted to you. And I will give you riches and wealth and honor, such as none of the kings who were before you has possessed nor those who will come after you.' So Solomon went from the high place which was at Gibeon, from the tent of meeting, to Jerusalem, and he reigned over Israel" (2 Ch. 1:7-13).

The Wisdom of Solomon

"Now when the queen of Sheba heard of the fame of Solomon, she came to Jerusalem to test Solomon with difficult questions. She had a very large retinue, with camels carrying spices and a large amount of gold and precious stones; and when she came to Solomon, she spoke with him about all that was on her heart. Solomon answered all her questions; nothing was hidden from Solomon which he did not explain to her. When the queen of Sheba had seen the wisdom of Solomon, the house which he had built, the food at his table, the seating of his servants, the attendance of his ministers and their attire, his cupbearers and their attire, and his stairway by which he went up to the house of the Lord, she was breathless. Then she said to the king, 'It was a true report which I heard in my own land about your words and your wisdom. Nevertheless I did not believe their reports until I came and my eyes had seen it. And behold, the half of the greatness of your wisdom was not told me. You surpass the report that I heard. How blessed are your men, how blessed are these your servants who stand before you continually and hear your wisdom. Blessed be the Lord your God who delighted in you, setting you on His throne as king for the Lord your God; because your God loved Israel establishing them forever, therefore He made you king over them, to do justice and righteousness.' Then she gave the king one hundred and twenty talents of gold and a very great amount of spices and precious stones; there had never been spice like that which the queen of Sheba gave to King Solomon" (2 Ch. 9:1-9).

Riches and Wisdom

"So King Solomon became greater than all the kings of the earth in riches and wisdom. And all the kings of the earth were seeking the presence of Solomon, to hear his wisdom which God had put in his heart. They brought every man his gift, articles of silver and gold, garments, weapons, spices, horses and mules, so much year by year" (2 Ch. 9:22-24).

WISDOM IN THE BOOK OF EZRA

According to the Wisdom of Your God

"You, Ezra, according to the wisdom of your God which is in your hand, appoint magistrates and judges that they may judge all the people who are in the province beyond the River, even all those who know the laws of your God; and you may teach anyone who is ignorant of them. Whoever will not observe the law of your God and the law of the king, let judgment be executed upon him strictly, whether for death or for banishment or for confiscation of goods or for imprisonment" (Ezr. 7:25-26).

Chapter Two

WISDOM IN THE BOOK OF JOB

They Die, Yet Without Wisdom

"Now a word was brought to me stealthily, And my ear received a whisper of it. Amid disquieting thoughts from the visions of the night, when deep sleep falls on men, dread came upon me, and trembling, and made all my bones shake. Then a spirit passed by my face; the hair of my flesh bristled up. It stood still, but I could not discern its appearance; a form was before my eyes; there was silence, then I heard a voice: 'Can mankind be just before God? Can a man be pure before his Maker? He puts no trust even in His servants; And against His angels He charges error. How much more those who dwell in houses of clay, Whose foundation is in the dust, Who are crushed before the moth! Between morning and evening they are broken in pieces; unobserved, they perish forever. Is not their tent-cord plucked up within them? They die, yet without wisdom'" (Job 4:12-21).

Show You the Secrets of Wisdom

"Then Zophar the Naamathite answered, 'Shall a multitude of words go unanswered, and a talkative man be acquitted? Shall your boasts silence men? And shall you scoff and none rebuke? For you have said, "My teaching is pure, and I am innocent in your eyes." But would that

God might speak, and open His lips against you, and show you the secrets of wisdom! For sound wisdom has two sides. Know then that God forgets a part of your iniquity'" (Job 11:1-6).

With You Wisdom Will Die

"Then Job responded, 'Truly then you are the people, and with you wisdom will die! But I have intelligence as well as you; I am not inferior to you. And who does not know such things as these? I am a joke to my friends, the one who called on God and He answered him; the just and blameless man is a joke. He who is at ease holds calamity in contempt, as prepared for those whose feet slip. The tents of the destroyers prosper, and those who provoke God are secure, whom God brings into their power'" (Job 12:1-6).

Wisdom Is With Aged Men

"But now ask the beasts, and let them teach you; and the birds of the heavens, and let them tell you. Or speak to the earth, and let it teach you; and let the fish of the sea declare to you. Who among all these does not know that the hand of the Lord has done this, in whose hand is the life of every living thing, and the breath of all mankind? Does not the ear test words, as the palate tastes its food? Wisdom is with aged men, with long life is understanding" (Job 12:7-12).

Chapter Two

With Him Are Wisdom and Might

"With Him are wisdom and might; to Him belong counsel and understanding. Behold, He tears down, and it cannot be rebuilt; He imprisons a man, and there can be no release. Behold, He restrains the waters, and they dry up; and He sends them out, and they inundate the earth. With Him are strength and sound wisdom, the misled and the misleader belong to Him. He makes counselors walk barefoot and makes fools of judges. He loosens the bond of kings and binds their loins with a girdle. He makes priests walk barefoot and overthrows the secure ones. He deprives the trusted ones of speech and takes away the discernment of the elders" (Job 12:13-20).

Become Your Wisdom

"But I would speak to the Almighty, and I desire to argue with God. But you smear with lies; you are all worthless physicians. O that you would be completely silent, and that it would become your wisdom! Please hear my argument and listen to the contentions of my lips. Will you speak what is unjust for God, and speak what is deceitful for Him? Will you show partiality for Him? Will you contend for God? Will it be well when He examines you? Or will you deceive Him as one deceives a man? He will surely reprove you If you secretly show partiality. Will not His majesty terrify you, and the dread of Him fall on you? Your memorable sayings are proverbs of ashes, your defenses are defenses of clay" (Job 13:3-12).

Limit Wisdom to Yourself

"Were you the first man to be born, or were you brought forth before the hills? Do you hear the secret counsel of God, and limit wisdom to yourself? What do you know that we do not know? What do you understand that we do not? Both the gray-haired and the aged are among us, older than your father. Are the consolations of God too small for you, even the word spoken gently with you? Why does your heart carry you away? And why do your eyes flash, that you should turn your spirit against God and allow such words to go out of your mouth? What is man, that he should be pure, or he who is born of a woman, that he should be righteous? Behold, He puts no trust in His holy ones, and the heavens are not pure in His sight; how much less one who is detestable and corrupt, Man, who drinks iniquity like water!" (Job 15:7-16).

Without Wisdom

"Then Job responded, 'What a help you are to the weak! How you have saved the arm without strength! What counsel you have given to one without wisdom! What helpful insight you have abundantly provided! To whom have you uttered words? And whose spirit was expressed through you?'" (Job 26:1-4).

Where Can Wisdom Be Found?

"But where can wisdom be found? And where is the place of understanding? Man does not know its value, nor is it found in the land of the living. The deep says, 'It is not in me'; and the sea says, 'It is not with me.' Pure gold cannot be given in exchange for it, nor can silver be weighed as its price. It cannot be valued in the gold of Ophir, in precious onyx, or sapphire. Gold or glass cannot equal it, nor can it be exchanged for articles of fine gold. Coral and crystal are not to be mentioned; and the acquisition of wisdom is above that of pearls. The topaz of Ethiopia cannot equal it, nor can it be valued in pure gold. Where then does wisdom come from? And where is the place of understanding? Thus it is hidden from the eyes of all living and concealed from the birds of the sky. Abaddon and Death say, 'With our ears we have heard a report of it'" (Job 28:12-22).

Behold, the Fear of the Lord, that Is Wisdom

"God understands its way, and He knows its place. For He looks to the ends of the earth and sees everything under the heavens. When He imparted weight to the wind and meted out the waters by measure, when He set a limit for the rain and a course for the thunderbolt, then He saw it and declared it; He established it and also searched it out. And to man He said, 'Behold, the fear of the Lord, that is wisdom; and to depart from evil is understanding'" (Job 28:23-28).

Increased Years Should Teach Wisdom

"So Elihu the son of Barachel the Buzite spoke out and said, 'I am young in years and you are old; therefore I was shy and afraid to tell you what I think. I thought age should speak, and increased years should teach wisdom. But it is a spirit in man, and the breath of the Almighty gives them understanding. The abundant in years may not be wise, nor may elders understand justice. So I say, "Listen to me, I too will tell what I think"'" (Job 32:6-10).

Do Not Say, We Have Found Wisdom

"Behold, I waited for your words, I listened to your reasonings, while you pondered what to say. I even paid close attention to you; indeed, there was no one who refuted Job, not one of you who answered his words. Do not say, 'We have found wisdom; God will rout him, not man.' For he has not arranged his words against me, nor will I reply to him with your arguments" (Job 32:11-14).

I Will Teach You Wisdom

"Behold, God does all these oftentimes with men, to bring back his soul from the pit, that he may be enlightened with the light of life. Pay attention, O Job, listen to me; keep silent, and let me speak. Then if you have anything to say, answer me; speak, for I desire to justify you. If not, listen to me; keep silent, and I will teach you wisdom" (Job 33:29-33).

His Words Are Without Wisdom

"For has anyone said to God, 'I have borne chastisement; I will not offend anymore; teach me what I do not see; if I have done iniquity, I will not do it again'? Shall He recompense on your terms, because you have rejected it? For you must choose, and not I; therefore declare what you know. Men of understanding will say to me, and a wise man who hears me, Job speaks without knowledge, and his words are without wisdom. Job ought to be tried to the limit, because he answers like wicked men. For he adds rebellion to his sin; he claps his hands among us, and multiplies his words against God" (Job 34:31-37).

Who Has Put Wisdom in the Innermost Being?

"Can you lift up your voice to the clouds, so that an abundance of water will cover you? Can you send forth lightnings that they may go and say to you, 'Here we are'? Who has put wisdom in the innermost being or given understanding to the mind? Who can count the clouds by wisdom, or tip the water jars of the heavens, when the dust hardens into a mass and the clods stick together?" (Job 38:34-38).

God Has Made Her Forget Wisdom

"The ostriches' wings flap joyously with the pinion and plumage of love, for she abandons her eggs to the earth and warms them in the dust, and she forgets that a foot may crush them, or that a wild beast may trample them. She treats her young cruelly, as if they were not hers; though her labor be in vain, she is unconcerned; because God has made her forget wisdom, and has not given her a share of understanding. When she lifts herself on high, she laughs at the horse and his rider" (Job 39:13-18).

WISDOM IN THE BOOK OF PSALMS

The Mouth of the Righteous Utters Wisdom

"Depart from evil and do good, so you will abide forever. For the Lord loves justice and does not forsake His godly ones; they are preserved forever, but the descendants of the wicked will be cut off. The righteous will inherit the land and dwell in it forever. The mouth of the righteous utters wisdom, and his tongue speaks justice. The law of his God is in his heart; his steps do not slip. The wicked spies upon the righteous and seeks to kill him. The Lord will not leave him in his hand or let him be condemned when he is judged. Wait for the Lord and keep His way, and He will exalt you to inherit the land; when the wicked are cut off, you will see it" (Ps. 37:27-34).

My Mouth Will Speak Wisdom

"Hear this, all peoples; Give ear, all inhabitants of the world, both low and high, Rich and poor together. My mouth will speak wisdom, and the meditation of my heart will be understanding. I will incline my ear to a proverb; I will express my riddle on the harp. Why should I fear in days of adversity, when the iniquity of my foes surrounds me, even those who trust in their wealth and boast in the abundance of their riches? No man can by any means redeem his brother or give to God a ransom for him—For the redemption of his soul is costly, And he should cease trying forever—That he should live on eternally, That he should not undergo decay" (Ps. 49:1-9).

You Will Make Me Know Wisdom

"Behold, I was brought forth in iniquity, and in sin my mother conceived me. Behold, You desire truth in the innermost being, and in the hidden part You will make me know wisdom.

Purify me with hyssop, and I shall be clean; wash me, and I shall be whiter than snow. Make me to hear joy and gladness, let the bones which You have broken rejoice. Hide Your face from my sins and blot out all my iniquities" (Ps. 51:5-9).

Present to You a Heart of Wisdom

"For we have been consumed by Your anger and by Your wrath we have been dismayed. You have placed our iniquities before You, our secret sins in the light of Your presence. For all our days have declined in Your fury; we have finished our years like a sigh. As for the days of our life, they contain seventy years, or if due to strength, eighty years, yet their pride is but labor and sorrow; For soon it is gone and we fly away. Who understands the power of Your anger And Your fury, according to the fear that is due You? So teach us to number our days, that we may present to You a heart of wisdom" (Ps. 90:7-12).

In Wisdom You Have Make All Your Works

"O Lord, how many are Your works! In wisdom You have made them all; the earth is full of Your possessions. There is the sea, great and broad, in which are swarms without number, animals both small and great. There the ships move along, and Leviathan, which You have formed to sport in it" (Ps. 104:24-26).

Teach His Elders Wisdom

"And He called for a famine upon the land; He broke the whole staff of bread. He sent a man before them, Joseph, who was sold as a slave. They afflicted his feet with fetters, he himself was laid in irons; until the time that his word came to pass, the word of the Lord tested him. The king sent and released him, the ruler of peoples, and set him free. He made him lord of his house And ruler over all his possessions, to imprison his princes at will, that he might teach his elders wisdom. Israel also came into Egypt; thus Jacob sojourned in the land of Ham. And He caused His people to be very fruitful, and made them stronger than their adversaries" (Ps. 105:16-24).

Fear of the Lord Is the Beginning of Wisdom

"The works of His hands are truth and justice; all His precepts are sure. They are upheld forever and ever; they are performed in truth and uprightness. He has sent redemption to His people; He has ordained His covenant forever; Holy and awesome is His name. The fear of the Lord is the beginning of wisdom; a good understanding have all those who do His commandments; His praise endures forever. Praise the Lord! How blessed is the man who fears the Lord, who greatly delights in His commandments. His descendants will be mighty on earth; the generation of the upright will be blessed. Wealth and riches are in his house, and his righteousness endures forever. Light arises in the darkness for the upright; He is gracious and compassionate and righteous. It is well with the man who is gracious and lends; He will maintain his cause in judgment. For he will never be shaken; the righteous will be remembered forever. He will not fear evil tidings; his heart is steadfast, trusting in the Lord. His heart is upheld, he will not fear, until he looks with satisfaction on his adversaries. He has given freely to the poor, His righteousness endures forever; His horn will be exalted in honor. The wicked will see it and be vexed, he will gnash his teeth and melt away; the desire of the wicked will perish" (Ps. 111:7-10).

WISDOM IN THE BOOK OF PROVERBS

To Know Wisdom and Instruction

"To know wisdom and instruction, to discern the sayings of understanding" (Pr. 1:2).

Fools Despise Wisdom and Instruction

"The fear of the Lord is the beginning of knowledge; Fools despise wisdom and instruction" (Pr. 1:7).

Wisdom Shouts in the Street

"Wisdom shouts in the street, she lifts her voice in the square" (Pr. 1:20).

Make Your Ear Attentive to Wisdom

"Make your ear attentive to wisdom, incline your heart to understanding" (Pr. 2:2).

The Lord Gives Wisdom

"For the Lord gives wisdom; from His mouth come knowledge and understanding" (Pr. 2:6).

He Stores Up Sound Wisdom for the Upright

"He stores up sound wisdom for the upright; He is a shield to those who walk in integrity" (Pr. 2:7).

Wisdom Will Enter Your Heart

"For wisdom will enter your heart and knowledge will be pleasant to your soul" (Pr. 2:10).

How Blessed Is the Man Who Finds Wisdom

"How blessed is the man who finds wisdom and the man who gains understanding" (Pr. 3:13).

The Lord by Wisdom Founded the Earth

"The Lord by wisdom founded the earth, by understanding He established the heavens" (Pr. 3:19).

Keep Sound Wisdom and Discretion

"My son, let them not vanish from your sight; keep sound wisdom and discretion" (Pr. 3:21).

Acquire Wisdom!

"Acquire wisdom! Acquire understanding! Do not forget nor turn away from the words of my mouth" (Pr. 4:5).

The Beginning of Wisdom Is: Acquire Wisdom!

"The beginning of wisdom is: Acquire wisdom; and with all your acquiring, get understanding" (Pr. 4:7).

In the Way of Wisdom

"I have directed you in the way of wisdom; I have led you in upright paths" (Pr. 4:11).

Give Attention to my Wisdom

"My son, give attention to my wisdom, incline your ear to my understanding" (Pr. 5:1).

Say to Wisdom, You Are My Sister

"Say to wisdom, "You are my sister," and call understanding your intimate friend" (Pr. 7:4).

Does Not Wisdom Call

"Does not wisdom call, and understanding lift up her voice?" (Pr. 8:1).

O Fools, Understand Wisdom

"O naive ones, understand prudence; and, O fools, understand wisdom" (Pr. 8:5).

Wisdom Is better than Jewels

"For wisdom is better than jewels; and all desirable things cannot compare with her" (Pr. 8:11).

I, Wisdom, Dwell with Prudence

"I, wisdom, dwell with prudence, and I find knowledge and discretion" (Pr. 8:12).

Counsel Is Mine and Sound Wisdom

"Counsel is mine and sound wisdom; I am understanding, power is mine" (Pr. 8:14).

Wisdom Has Built Her House

"Wisdom has built her house; she has hewn out her seven pillars" (Pr. 9:1).

Fear of the Lord Is the Beginning of Wisdom

"The fear of the Lord is the beginning of wisdom, and the knowledge of the Holy One is understanding" (Pr. 9:10).

On the Lips of the Discerning, Wisdom Is Found

"On the lips of the discerning, wisdom is found, but a rod is for the back of him who lacks understanding" (Pr. 10:13).

Wisdom to a Man of Understanding

"Doing wickedness is like sport to a fool, and so is wisdom to a man of understanding" (Pr. 10:23).

Flows with Wisdom

"The mouth of the righteous flows with wisdom, But the perverted tongue will be cut out" (Pr. 10:31).

With the Humble Is Wisdom

"He who despises his neighbor lacks sense, but a man of understanding keeps silent" (Pr. 11:2).

Wisdom Is with Those Who Receive Counsel

"Through insolence comes nothing but strife, but wisdom is with those who receive counsel" (Pr. 13:10).

A Scoffer Seeks Wisdom and Finds None

"A scoffer seeks wisdom and finds none, but knowledge is easy to one who has understanding" (Pr. 14:6).

Wisdom of the Sensible

"The wisdom of the sensible is to understand his way, but the foolishness of fools is deceit" (Pr. 14:8).

Wisdom Rests in the Heart

"Wisdom rests in the heart of one who has understanding, but in the hearts of fools it is made known" (Pr. 14:33).

The Instruction for Wisdom

"The fear of the Lord is the instruction for wisdom, and before honor comes humility" (Pr. 15:33).

Better It Is to Get Wisdom than Gold

"How much better it is to get wisdom than gold! And to get understanding is to be chosen above silver" (Pr. 16:16).

A Fool to Buy Wisdom

"Why is there a price in the hand of a fool to buy wisdom, when he has no sense?" (Pr. 17:16).

Wisdom Is

"Wisdom is in the presence of the one who has understanding, but the eyes of a fool are on the ends of the earth" (Pr. 17:24).

Quarrels Against All Sound Wisdom

"He who separates himself seeks his own desire, he quarrels against all sound wisdom" (Pr. 18:1).

The Fountain of Wisdom Is a Bubbling Brook

"The words of a man's mouth are deep waters; the fountain of wisdom is a bubbling brook" (Pr. 18:4).

He Who Gets Wisdom Loves His Own Soul

"He who gets wisdom loves his own soul; he who keeps understanding will find good" (Pr. 19:8).

No Wisdom

"There is no wisdom and no understanding and no counsel against the Lord" (Pr. 21:30).

He Will Despise the Wisdom of Your Words

"Do not speak in the hearing of a fool, for he will despise the wisdom of your words" (Pr. 23:9).

Get Wisdom and Instruction and Understanding

"Buy truth, and do not sell it, get wisdom and instruction and understanding" (Pr. 23:23).

By Wisdom a House Is Built

"By wisdom a house is built and by understanding it is established" (Pr. 24:3).

Wisdom Is Too Exalted for a Fool

"Wisdom is too exalted for a fool, he does not open his mouth in the gate" (Pr. 24:7).

Know that Wisdom Is Thus for Your Soul

"Know that wisdom is thus for your soul; if you find it, then there will be a future, and your hope will not be cut off" (Pr. 24:14).

A Man Who Loves Wisdom Makes His Father Glad

"A man who loves wisdom makes his father glad, but he who keeps company with harlots wastes his wealth" (Pr. 29:3).

The Rod and Reproof Give Wisdom

"The rod and reproof give wisdom, but a child who gets his own way brings shame to his mother" (Pr. 29:15).

Neither Gave I Learned Wisdom

"Neither have I learned wisdom, nor do I have the knowledge of the Holy One" (Pr. 30:3).

She Opens Her Mouth in Wisdom

"She opens her mouth in wisdom, and the teaching of kindness is on her tongue" (Pr. 31:26).

WISDOM IN THE BOOK OF ECCLESIASTES

I Set My Mind to Seek and Explore by Wisdom

"I, the Preacher, have been king over Israel in Jerusalem. And I set my mind to seek and explore by wisdom concerning all that has been done under heaven. It is a grievous task which God has given to the sons of men to be afflicted with. I have seen all the works which have been done under the sun, and behold, all is vanity and striving after wind. What is crooked cannot be straightened and what is lacking cannot be counted" (Ecc. 1:12-15).

In Much Wisdom There Is Much Grief

"I said to myself, 'Behold, I have magnified and increased wisdom more than all who were over Jerusalem before me; and my mind has observed a wealth of wisdom and knowledge.' And I set my mind to know wisdom and to know madness and folly; I realized that this also is striving after wind. Because in much wisdom there is much grief, and increasing knowledge results in increasing pain" (Ecc. 1:16-18).

My Wisdom Also Stood by Me

"Then I became great and increased more than all who preceded me in Jerusalem. My wisdom also stood by me. All that my eyes desired I did not refuse them. I did not withhold my heart from any pleasure, for my heart was pleased because of all my labor and this was my reward for all my labor. Thus I considered all my activities which my hands had done and the labor which I had exerted, and behold all was vanity and striving after wind and there was no profit under the sun" (Ecc. 2:9-11).

Wisdom Excels Folly as Light Excels Darkness

"So I turned to consider wisdom, madness and folly; for what will the man do who will come after the king except what has already been done? And I saw that wisdom excels folly as light excels darkness. The wise man's eyes are in his head, but the fool walks in darkness. And yet I know that one fate befalls them both. Then I said to myself, 'As is the fate of the fool, it will also befall me. Why then have I been extremely wise?' So I said to myself, 'This too is vanity.' For there is no lasting remembrance of the wise man as with the fool, inasmuch as in the coming days all will be forgotten. And how the wise man and the fool alike die! So I hated life, for the work which had been done under the sun was grievous to me; because everything is futility and striving after wind" (Ecc. 2:12-17).

Who Has Labored with Wisdom

"Thus I hated all the fruit of my labor for which I had labored under the sun, for I must leave it to the man who will come after me. And who knows whether he will be a wise man or a fool? Yet he will have control over all the fruit of my labor for which I have labored by acting wisely under the sun. This too is vanity. Therefore I completely despaired of all the fruit of my labor for which I had labored under the sun. When there is a man who has labored with wisdom, knowledge and skill, then he gives his legacy to one who has not labored with them. This too is vanity and a great evil. For what does a man get in all his labor and in his striving with which he labors under the sun? Because all his days his task is painful and grievous; even at night his mind does not rest. This too is vanity" (Ecc. 2:18-23).

He Has Given Wisdom and Knowledge and Joy

"There is nothing better for a man than to eat and drink and tell himself that his labor is good. This also I have seen that it is from the hand of God. For who can eat and who can have enjoyment without Him? For to a person who is good in His sight He has given wisdom and knowledge and joy, while to the sinner He has given the task of gathering and collecting so that he may give to one who is good in God's sight. This too is vanity and striving after wind" (Ecc. 2:24-26).

Wisdom Is Protection

"A good name is better than a good ointment, and the day of one's death is better than the day of one's birth. It is better to go to a house of mourning than to go to a house of feasting, because that is the end of every man, and the living takes it to heart. Sorrow is better than laughter, for when a face is sad a heart may be happy. The mind of the wise is in the house of mourning, while the mind of fools is in the house of pleasure. It is better to listen to the rebuke of a wise man than for one to listen to the song of fools. For as the crackling of thorn bushes under a pot, so is the laughter of the fool; and this too is futility. For oppression makes a wise man mad, and a bribe corrupts the heart. The end of a matter is better than its beginning; patience of spirit is better than haughtiness of spirit. Do not be eager in your heart to be angry, for anger resides in the bosom of fools. Do not say, 'Why is it that the former days were better than these?' For it is not from wisdom that you ask about this. Wisdom along with an inheritance is good and an advantage to those who see the sun. For wisdom is protection just as money is protection, but the advantage of knowledge is that wisdom preserves the lives of its possessors. Consider the work of God, for who is able to straighten what He has bent? In the day of prosperity be happy, but in the day of adversity consider — God has made the one as well as the other so that man will not discover anything that will be after him" (Ecc. 7:1-14).

Wisdom Strengthens a Wise Man

"Wisdom strengthens a wise man more than ten rulers who are in a city. Indeed, there is not a righteous man on earth who continually does good and who never sins. Also, do not take seriously all words which are spoken, so that you will not hear your servant cursing you. For you also have realized that you likewise have many times cursed others" (Ecc. 7:19-22).

I Tested All This with Wisdom

"I tested all this with wisdom, and I said, 'I will be wise,' but it was far from me. What has been is remote and exceedingly mysterious. Who can discover it? I directed my mind to know, to investigate and to seek wisdom and an explanation, and to know the evil of folly and the foolishness of madness. And I discovered more bitter than death the woman whose heart is snares and nets, whose hands are chains. One who is pleasing to God will escape from her, but the sinner will be captured by her" (Ecc. 7:23-26).

A Man's Wisdom Illumines Him

"Who is like the wise man and who knows the interpretation of a matter? A man's wisdom illumines him and causes his stern face to beam" (Ecc. 8:1).

I Gave My Heart to Know Wisdom

"When I gave my heart to know wisdom and to see the task which has been done on the earth (even though one should never sleep day or night), and I saw every work of God, I concluded that man cannot discover the work which has been done under the sun. Even though man should seek laboriously, he will not discover; and though the wise man should say, 'I know,' he cannot discover" (Ecc. 8:16-17).

There Is No Wisdom in Sheol

"Whatever your hand finds to do, do it with all your might; for there is no activity or planning or knowledge or wisdom in Sheol where you are going" (Ecc. 9:10).

Wisdom Is Better than Weapons of War

"Also this I came to see as wisdom under the sun, and it impressed me. There was a small city with few men in it and a great king came to it, surrounded it and constructed large siegeworks against it. But there was found in it a poor wise man and he delivered the city by his wisdom. Yet no one remembered that poor man. So I said, "Wisdom is better than strength." But the wisdom of the poor man is despised and his words are not heeded. The words of the wise heard in quietness are better than the shouting of a ruler among fools. Wisdom is better than weapons of war, but one sinner destroys much good" (Ecc. 9:13-18).

Foolishness Is Weightier than Wisdom and Honor

"Dead flies make a perfumer's oil stink, so a little foolishness is weightier than wisdom and honor. A wise man's heart directs him toward the right, but the foolish man's heart directs him toward the left. Even when the fool walks along the road, his sense is lacking and he demonstrates to everyone that he is a fool. If the ruler's temper rises against you, do not abandon your position, because composure allays great offenses" (Ecc. 10:1-4).

Wisdom Has the Advantage of Giving Success

"He who digs a pit may fall into it, and a serpent may bite him who breaks through a wall. He who quarries stones may be hurt by them, and he who splits logs may be endangered by them. If the axe is dull and he does not sharpen its edge, then he must exert more strength. Wisdom has the advantage of giving success. If the serpent bites before being charmed, there is no profit for the charmer. Words from the mouth of a wise man are gracious, while the lips of a fool consume him; the beginning of his talking is folly and the end of it is wicked madness. Yet the fool multiplies words. No man knows what will happen, and who can tell him what will come after him? The toil of a fool so wearies him that he does not even know how to go to a city. Woe to you, O land, whose king is a lad and whose princes feast in the morning. Blessed are you, O land, whose king is of nobility and whose princes eat at the appropriate time—for strength and not for drunkenness. Through indolence the rafters sag, and through slackness the house leaks. Men prepare a meal for enjoyment, and wine makes life merry, and money is the answer to everything. Furthermore, in your bedchamber do not curse a king, and in your sleeping rooms do not curse a rich man, for a bird of the heavens will carry the sound and the winged creature will make the matter known"(Ecc. 10:8-20).

WISDOM IN THE BOOK OF ISAIAH

By the Power of My Hand and by My Wisdom

"So it will be that when the Lord has completed all His work on Mount Zion and on Jerusalem, He will say, 'I will punish the fruit of the arrogant heart of the king of Assyria and the pomp of his haughtiness.' For he has said, 'By the power of my hand and by my wisdom I did this, for I have understanding; and I removed the boundaries of the peoples and plundered their treasures, and like a mighty man I brought down their inhabitants, and my hand reached to the riches of the peoples like a nest, and as one gathers abandoned eggs, I gathered all the earth; And there was not one that flapped its wing or opened its beak or chirped'" (Is. 10:12-14).

The Spirit of Wisdom and Understanding

"Then a shoot will spring from the stem of Jesse, and a branch from his roots will bear fruit. The Spirit of the Lord will rest on Him, the spirit of wisdom and understanding, the spirit of counsel and strength, the spirit of knowledge and the fear of the Lord. And He will delight in the fear of the Lord, and He will not judge by what His eyes see, nor make a decision by what His ears hear; but with righteousness He will judge the poor, and decide with fairness for the afflicted of the earth; and He will strike the earth with the rod of His mouth, and with the breath of His lips He will slay the wicked. Also righteousness will be the belt about His loins, and faithfulness the belt about His waist" (Is. 11:1-5).

Who Has Made His Wisdom Great

"Give ear and hear my voice, listen and hear my words. Does the farmer plow continually to plant seed? Does he continually turn and harrow the ground? Does he not level its surface and sow dill and scatter cummin and plant wheat in rows, barley in its place and rye within its area? For his God instructs and teaches him properly. For dill is not threshed with a threshing sledge, nor is the cartwheel driven over cummin; but dill is beaten out with a rod, and cummin with a club. Grain for bread is crushed, indeed, he does not continue to thresh it forever. Because the wheel of his cart and his horses eventually damage it, he does not thresh it longer. This also comes from the Lord of hosts, who has made His counsel wonderful and His wisdom great" (Is. 28:23-29).

Chapter Two

The Wisdom of Their Wise Men Will Perish

"Then the Lord said, 'Because this people draw near with their words and honor Me with their lip service, but they remove their hearts far from Me, and their reverence for Me consists of tradition learned by rote, therefore behold, I will once again deal marvelously with this people, wondrously marvelous; and the wisdom of their wise men will perish, and the discernment of their discerning men will be concealed'" (Is. 29:13-14).

A Wealth of Salvation, Wisdom and Knowledge

"Woe to you, O destroyer, while you were not destroyed; and he who is treacherous, while others did not deal treacherously with him. As soon as you finish destroying, you will be destroyed; as soon as you cease to deal treacherously, others will deal treacherously with you. O Lord, be gracious to us; we have waited for You. Be their strength every morning, our salvation also in the time of distress. At the sound of the tumult peoples flee; at the lifting up of Yourself nations disperse. Your spoil is gathered as the caterpillar gathers; as locusts rushing about men rush about on it. The Lord is exalted, for He dwells on high; He has filled Zion with justice and righteousness. And He will be the stability of your times, a wealth of salvation, wisdom and knowledge; the fear of the Lord is his treasure. Behold, their brave men cry in the streets, the ambassadors of peace weep bitterly. The highways are desolate, the traveler has ceased, He has broken the covenant, he has despised the cities, He has no regard for man. The land mourns and pines away, Lebanon is shamed and withers; Sharon is like a desert plain, and Bashan and Carmel lose their foliage. 'Now I will arise,' says the Lord, 'Now I will be exalted, now I will be lifted up. You have conceived chaff, you will give birth to stubble; My breath will consume you like a fire. The peoples will be burned to lime, Like cut thorns which are burned in the fire'" (Is. 33:1-12).

Your Wisdom and Your Knowledge

"Now, then, hear this, you sensual one, who dwells securely, who says in your heart, 'I am, and there is no one besides me. I will not sit as a widow, nor know loss of children.' But these two things will come on you suddenly in one day: loss of children and widowhood. They will come on you in full measure In spite of your many sorceries, In spite of the great power of your spells. You felt secure in your wickedness and said, 'No one sees me,' Your wisdom and your knowledge, they have deluded you; For you have said in your heart, 'I am, and there is no one besides me.' But evil will come on you which you will not know how to charm away; and disaster will fall on you for which you cannot atone; and destruction about which you do not know will come on you suddenly" (Is. 47:8-11).

WISDOM IN THE BOOK OF JEREMIAH

What Kind of Wisdom Do They Have?

"How can you say, 'We are wise, and the law of the Lord is with us'? But behold, the lying pen of the scribes has made it into a lie. The wise men are put to shame, they are dismayed and caught; behold, they have rejected the word of the Lord, and what kind of wisdom do they have? Therefore I will give their wives to others, their fields to new owners; because from the least even to the greatest everyone is greedy for gain; from the prophet even to the priest everyone practices deceit. They heal the brokenness of the daughter of My people superficially, saying, 'Peace, peace,' But there is no peace. Were they ashamed because of the abomination they had done? They certainly were not ashamed, and they did not know how to blush; therefore they shall fall among those who fall; at the time of their punishment they shall be brought down," Says the Lord" (Jer. 8:8-12).

Let Not a Wise Man Boast of His Wisdom

"Thus says the Lord, 'Let not a wise man boast of his wisdom, and let not the mighty man boast of his might, let not a rich man boast of his riches; but let him who boasts boast of this, that he understands and knows Me, that I am the Lord who exercises lovingkindness, justice and righteousness on earth; for I delight in these things,' declares the Lord" (Jer. 9:23-24).

Who Established the World by His Wisdom

"It is He who made the earth by His power, who established the world by His wisdom; and by His understanding He has stretched out the heavens. When He utters His voice, there is a tumult of waters in the heavens, and He causes the clouds to ascend from the end of the earth; He makes lightning for the rain, and brings out the wind from His storehouses. Every man is stupid, devoid of knowledge; every goldsmith is put to shame by his idols; for his molten images are deceitful, and there is no breath in them. They are worthless, a work of mockery; in the time of their punishment they will perish. The portion of Jacob is not like these; for the Maker of all is He, and Israel is the tribe of His inheritance; the Lord of hosts is His name" (Jer. 10:12-16).

Has Their Wisdom Decayed?

"Concerning Edom. Thus says the Lord of hosts, 'Is there no longer any wisdom in Teman? Has good counsel been lost to the prudent? Has their wisdom decayed? Flee away, turn back, dwell in the depths, O inhabitants of Dedan, for I will bring the disaster of Esau upon him at the time I punish him. If grape gatherers came to you, would they not leave gleanings? If thieves came by night, they would destroy only until they had enough. But I have stripped Esau bare, I have uncovered his hiding places So that he will not be able to conceal himself; his offspring has been destroyed along with his relatives and his neighbors, and he is no more. Leave your orphans behind, I will keep them alive; and let your widows trust in Me'" (Jer. 49:7-11).

Who Established the World by His Wisdom

"It is He who made the earth by His power, who established the world by His wisdom, and by His understanding He stretched out the heavens. When He utters His voice, there is a tumult of waters in the heavens, and He causes the clouds to ascend from the end of the earth; He makes lightning for the rain and brings forth the wind from His storehouses. All mankind is stupid, devoid of knowledge; every goldsmith is put to shame by his idols, for his molten images are deceitful, and there is no breath in them. They are worthless, a work of mockery; in the time of their punishment they will perish. The portion of Jacob is not like these; for the Maker of all is He, and of the tribe of His inheritance; the Lord of hosts is His name. He says, 'You are My war-club, My weapon of war; And with you I shatter nations, And with you I destroy kingdoms. With you I shatter the horse and his rider, and with you I shatter the chariot and its rider, and with you I shatter man and woman, and with you I shatter old man and youth, and with you I shatter young man and virgin, and with you I shatter the shepherd and his flock, and with you I shatter the farmer and his team, and with you I shatter governors and prefects'" (Jer. 51:15-23).

WISDOM IN THE BOOK OF EZEKIEL

By Your Wisdom You Have Acquired Riches

"The word of the Lord came again to me, saying, 'Son of man, say to the leader of Tyre, "Thus says the Lord God, 'Because your heart is lifted up and you have said, "I am a god, I sit in the seat of gods In the heart of the seas"; Yet you are a man and not God, although you make your heart like the heart of God—behold, you are wiser than Daniel; there is no secret that is a match for you. By your wisdom and understanding you have acquired riches for yourself and have acquired gold and silver for your treasuries. By your great wisdom, by your trade You have increased your riches and your heart is lifted up because of your riches—therefore thus says the Lord God, "Because you have made your heart like the heart of God, therefore, behold, I will bring strangers upon you, the most ruthless of the nations. And they will draw their swords against the beauty of your wisdom and defile your splendor. They will bring you down to the pit, and you will die the death of those who are slain In the heart of the seas. Will you still say, "I am a god,"

In the presence of your slayer, though you are a man and not God, in the hands of those who wound you? You will die the death of the uncircumcised by the hand of strangers, for I have spoken!' declares the Lord God!'"'" (Eze. 28:1-10).

Full of Wisdom and Perfect in Beauty

"Again the word of the Lord came to me saying, 'Son of man, take up a lamentation over the king of Tyre and say to him, "Thus says the Lord God, 'You had the seal of perfection, full of wisdom and perfect in beauty. You were in Eden, the garden of God; every precious stone was your covering: the ruby, the topaz and the diamond; the beryl, the onyx and the jasper; the lapis lazuli, the turquoise and the emerald; and the gold, the workmanship of your settings and sockets, was in you. On the day that you were created They were prepared. You were the anointed cherub who covers, and I placed you there. You were on the holy mountain of God; you walked in the midst of the stones of fire. You were blameless in your ways from the day you were created until unrighteousness was found in you. By the abundance of your trade you were internally filled with violence, and you sinned; therefore I have cast you as profane from the mountain of God. And I have destroyed you, O covering cherub, from the midst of the stones of fire. Your heart was lifted up because of your beauty; you corrupted your wisdom by reason of your splendor. I cast you to the ground; I put you before kings, that they may see you. By the multitude of your iniquities, in the unrighteousness of your trade you profaned your sanctuaries. Therefore I have brought fire from the midst of you; it has consumed you, and I have turned you to ashes on the earth in the eyes of all who see you. All who know you among the peoples are appalled at you; you have become terrified and you will cease to be forever'"'" (Eze. 28:11-19).

WISDOM IN THE BOOK OF DANIEL

Showing Intelligence in Every Branch of Wisdom

"Then the king ordered Ashpenaz, the chief of his officials, to bring in some of the sons of Israel, including some of the royal family and of the nobles, youths in whom was no defect, who were good-looking, showing intelligence in every branch of wisdom, endowed with understanding and discerning knowledge, and who had ability for serving in the king's court; and he ordered him to teach them the literature and language of the Chaldeans. The king appointed for them a daily ration from the king's choice food and from the wine which he drank, and appointed that they should be educated three years, at the end of which they were to enter the king's personal service. Now among them from the sons of Judah were Daniel, Hananiah, Mishael and Azariah. Then the commander of the officials assigned new names to them; and to Daniel he assigned the name Belteshazzar, to Hananiah Shadrach, to Mishael Meshach and to Azariah Abed-nego" (Da. 1:3-7).

Intelligence in Every Branch of Literature and Wisdom

"As for these four youths, God gave them knowledge and intelligence in every branch of literature and wisdom; Daniel even understood all kinds of visions and dreams" (Da. 1:17).

For Every Matter of Wisdom and Understanding

"Then at the end of the days which the king had specified for presenting them, the commander of the officials presented them before Nebuchadnezzar. The king talked with them, and out of them all not one was found like Daniel, Hananiah, Mishael and Azariah; so they entered the king's personal service. As for every matter of wisdom and understanding about which the king consulted them, he found them ten times better than all the magicians and conjurers who were in all his realm. And Daniel continued until the first year of Cyrus the king" (Da. 1:18-21).

For Wisdom and Power Belong to Him

"Then the mystery was revealed to Daniel in a night vision. Then Daniel blessed the God of heaven; Daniel said, 'Let the name of God be blessed forever and ever, for wisdom and power belong to Him. It is He who changes the times and the epochs; He removes kings and establishes kings; He gives wisdom to wise men and knowledge to men of understanding. It is He who reveals the profound and hidden things; He knows what is in the darkness, and the light dwells with Him. To You, O God of my fathers, I give thanks and praise, for You have given me wisdom and power; even now you have made known to me what we requested of You, for You have made known to us the king's matter'" (Da. 2:19-23).

Any Wisdom Residing in Me

"Then Arioch hurriedly brought Daniel into the king's presence and spoke to him as follows: 'I have found a man among the exiles from Judah who can make the interpretation known to the king!' The king said to Daniel, whose name was Belteshazzar, 'Are you able to make known to me the dream which I have seen and its interpretation?' Daniel answered before the king and said, 'As for the mystery about which the king has inquired, neither wise men, conjurers, magicians nor diviners are able to declare it to the king. However, there is a God in heaven who reveals mysteries, and He has made known to King Nebuchadnezzar what will take place in the latter days. This was your dream and the visions in your mind while on your bed. As for you, O king, while on your bed your thoughts turned to what would take place in the future; and He who reveals mysteries has made known to you what will take place. But as for me, this mystery has not been revealed to me for any wisdom residing in me more than in any other living man, but for the purpose of making the interpretation known to the king, and that you may understand the thoughts of your mind'" (Da. 2:25-30).

Illumination, Insight and Wisdom

"The queen entered the banquet hall because of the words of the king and his nobles; the queen spoke and said, 'O king, live forever! Do not let your thoughts alarm you or your face be pale. There is a man in your kingdom in whom is a spirit of the holy gods; and in the days of your father, illumination, insight and wisdom like the wisdom of the gods were found in him. And King Nebuchadnezzar, your father, your father the king, appointed him chief of the magicians, conjurers, Chaldeans and diviners. This was because an extraordinary spirit, knowledge and insight, interpretation of dreams, explanation of enigmas and solving of difficult problems were found in this Daniel, whom the king named

Belteshazzar. Let Daniel now be summoned and he will declare the interpretation'" (Da. 5:10-12).

Extraordinary Wisdom Have Been Found in You

"Then Daniel was brought in before the king. The king spoke and said to Daniel, "Are you that Daniel who is one of the exiles from Judah, whom my father the king brought from Judah? Now I have heard about you that a spirit of the gods is in you, and that illumination, insight and extraordinary wisdom have been found in you. Just now the wise men and the conjurers were brought in before me that they might read this inscription and make its interpretation known to me, but they could not declare the interpretation of the message. But I personally have heard about you, that you are able to give interpretations and solve difficult problems. Now if you are able to read the inscription and make its interpretation known to me, you will be clothed with purple and wear a necklace of gold around your neck, and you will have authority as the third ruler in the kingdom"" (Da. 5:13-16).

WISDOM IN THE BOOK OF MICAH

It Is Sound Wisdom to Fear Your Name

"The voice of the Lord will call to the city — and it is sound wisdom to fear Your name: 'Hear, O tribe. Who has appointed its time? Is there yet a man in the wicked house, Along with treasures of wickedness And a short measure that is cursed? Can I justify wicked scales And a bag of deceptive weights? For the rich men of the city are full of violence, Her residents speak lies, And their tongue is deceitful in their mouth. So also I will make you sick, striking you down, Desolating you because of your sins. You will eat, but you will not be satisfied, and your vileness will be in your midst. You will try to remove for safekeeping, but you will not preserve anything, and what you do preserve I will give to the sword. You will sow but you will not reap. You will tread the olive but will not anoint yourself with oil; and the grapes, but you will not drink wine. The statutes of Omri and all the works of the house of Ahab are observed; and in their devices you walk. Therefore I will give you up for destruction and your inhabitants for derision, and you will bear the reproach of My people'" (Mic. 6:9-16).

WISDOM IN THE NEW TESTAMENT

WISDOM IN THE BOOK OF MATTHEW

Wisdom Is vindicated by Her Deeds

"But to what shall I compare this generation? It is like children sitting in the market places, who call out to the other children, and say, 'We played the flute for you, and you did not dance; we sang a dirge, and you did not mourn.' For John came neither eating nor drinking, and they say, 'He has a demon!' The Son of Man came eating and drinking, and they say, 'Behold, a gluttonous man and a drunkard, a friend of tax collectors and sinners!' Yet wisdom is vindicated by her deeds" (Mt. 11:16-19).

The Ends of the Earth to Hear the Wisdom

"Then some of the scribes and Pharisees said to Him, 'Teacher, we want to see a sign from You.' But He answered and said to them, 'An evil and adulterous generation craves for a sign; and yet no sign will be given to it but the sign of Jonah the prophet; for just as JONAH WAS THREE DAYS AND THREE NIGHTS IN THE BELLY OF THE SEA MONSTER, so will the Son of Man be three days and three nights in the heart of the earth. The men of Nineveh will stand up with this generation at the judgment, and will condemn it because they repented at the preaching of Jonah;

and behold, something greater than Jonah is here. The Queen of the South will rise up with this generation at the judgment and will condemn it, because she came from the ends of the earth to hear the wisdom of Solomon; and behold, something greater than Solomon is here'" (Mt. 12:38-42).

Where Did This Man Get This Wisdom

"When Jesus had finished these parables, He departed from there. He came to His hometown and began teaching them in their synagogue, so that they were astonished, and said, 'Where did this man get this wisdom and these miraculous powers? Is not this the carpenter's son? Is not His mother called Mary, and His brothers, James and Joseph and Simon and Judas? And His sisters, are they not all with us? Where then did this man get all these things?' And they took offense at Him. But Jesus said to them, 'A prophet is not without honor except in his hometown and in his own household.' And He did not do many miracles there because of their unbelief" (Mt. 13:53-58).

WISDOM IN THE BOOK OF MARK

What Is This Wisdom Given to Him

"Jesus went out from there and came into His hometown; and His disciples followed Him.

When the Sabbath came, He began to teach in the synagogue; and the many listeners were astonished, saying, "Where did this man get these things, and what is this wisdom given to Him, and such miracles as these performed by His hands? Is not this the carpenter, the son of Mary, and brother of James and Joses and Judas and Simon? Are not His sisters here with us?" And they took offense at Him. Jesus said to them, "A prophet is not without honor except in his hometown and among his own relatives and in his own household." And He could do no miracle there except that He laid His hands on a few sick people and healed them. And He wondered at their unbelief. And He was going around the villages teaching. (Mk. 6:1-6).

WISDOM IN THE BOOK OF LUKE

To Grow and Become Strong, Increasing in Wisdom

"When they had performed everything according to the Law of the Lord, they returned to Galilee, to their own city of Nazareth. The Child continued to grow and become strong, increasing in wisdom; and the grace of God was upon Him" (Lk. 2:39-40).

Kept Increasing in Wisdom and Stature

"And Jesus kept increasing in wisdom and stature, and in favor with God and men" (Lk. 2:52).

Yet Wisdom Is Vindicated by All Her Children

"To what then shall I compare the men of this generation, and what are they like? They are like children who sit in the market place and call to one another, and they say, 'We played the flute for you, and you did not dance; we sang a dirge, and you did not weep.' For John the Baptist has come eating no bread and drinking no wine, and you say, 'He has a demon!' The Son of Man has come eating and drinking, and you say, 'Behold, a gluttonous man and a drunkard, a friend of tax collectors and sinners!' Yet wisdom is vindicated by all her children" (Lk. 7:31-35).

The Wisdom of God

"One of the lawyers said to Him in reply, 'Teacher, when You say this, You insult us too.' But He said, 'Woe to you lawyers as well! For you weigh men down with burdens hard to bear, while you yourselves will not even touch the burdens with one of your fingers. Woe to you! For you build the tombs of the prophets, and it was your fathers who killed them. So you are witnesses and approve the deeds of your fathers;

because it was they who killed them, and you build their tombs. For this reason also the wisdom of God said, 'I will send to them prophets and apostles, and some of them they will kill and some they will persecute, so that the blood of all the prophets, shed since the foundation of the world, may be charged against this generation, from the blood of Abel to the blood of Zechariah, who was killed between the altar and the house of God; yes, I tell you, it shall be charged against this generation." Woe to you lawyers! For you have taken away the key of knowledge; you yourselves did not enter, and you hindered those who were entering'" (Lk. 11:45-52).

I Will Give You Utterance and Wisdom

"But before all these things, they will lay their hands on you and will persecute you, delivering you to the synagogues and prisons, bringing you before kings and governors for My name's sake. It will lead to an opportunity for your testimony. So make up your minds not to prepare beforehand to defend yourselves; for I will give you utterance and wisdom which none of your opponents will be able to resist or refute. But you will be betrayed even by parents and brothers and relatives and friends, and they will put some of you to death, and you will be hated by all because of My name. Yet not a hair of your head will perish. By your endurance you will gain your lives" (Lk. 21:12-19).

WISDOM IN THE BOOK OF ACTS

Full of the Spirit and of Wisdom

"Now at this time while the disciples were increasing in number, a complaint arose on the part of the Hellenistic Jews against the native Hebrews, because their widows were being overlooked in the daily serving of food. So the twelve summoned the congregation of the disciples and said, 'It is not desirable for us to neglect the word of God in order to serve tables. Therefore, brethren, select from among you seven men of good reputation, full of the Spirit and of wisdom, whom we may put in charge of this task. But we will devote ourselves to prayer and to the ministry of the word.' The statement found approval with the whole congregation; and they chose Stephen, a man full of faith and of the Holy Spirit, and Philip, Prochorus, Nicanor, Timon, Parmenas and Nicolas, a proselyte from Antioch. And these they brought before the apostles; and after praying, they laid their hands on them" (Ac. 6:1-6).

They Were Unable to Cope with the Wisdom

"And Stephen, full of grace and power, was performing great wonders and signs among the people. But some men from what was called the Synagogue of the Freedmen, including both Cyrenians and Alexandrians, and some from

Cilicia and Asia, rose up and argued with Stephen. But they were unable to cope with the wisdom and the Spirit with which he was speaking. Then they secretly induced men to say, 'We have heard him speak blasphemous words against Moses and against God.' And they stirred up the people, the elders and the scribes, and they came up to him and dragged him away and brought him before the Council. They put forward false witnesses who said, 'This man incessantly speaks against this holy place and the Law; for we have heard him say that this Nazarene, Jesus, will destroy this place and alter the customs which Moses handed down to us'" (Ac. 6:8-14).

Granted Him Favor and Wisdom

"The patriarchs became jealous of Joseph and sold him into Egypt. Yet God was with him, and rescued him from all his afflictions, and granted him favor and wisdom in the sight of Pharaoh, king of Egypt, and he made him governor over Egypt and all his household" (Ac. 7:9-10).

WISDOM IN THE BOOK OF ROMANS

The Riches Both of Wisdom and Knowledge

"Oh, the depth of the riches both of the wisdom and knowledge of God! How unsearchable are His judgments and unfathomable His ways! For WHO HAS KNOWN THE MIND OF THE LORD, OR WHO BECAME HIS COUNSELOR? Or WHO HAS FIRST GIVEN TO HIM THAT IT MIGHT BE PAID BACK TO HIM AGAIN? For from Him and through Him and to Him are all things. To Him be the glory forever. Amen!" (Ro. 11:33-36).

WISDOM IN THE BOOK OF 1 CORINTHIANS

Not With Wisdom of Words

"Now I plead with you, brethren, by the name of our Lord Jesus Christ, that you all speak the same thing, and that there be no divisions among you, but that you be perfectly joined together in the same mind and in the same judgment. For it has been declared to me concerning you, my brethren, by those of Chloe's household, that there are contentions among you. Now I say this, that each of you says, 'I am of Paul,' or 'I am of Apollos,' or 'I am of Cephas,' or 'I am of Christ.' Is Christ divided? Was Paul crucified for you? Or were you baptized in the name of Paul? I thank God that I baptized none of you except Crispus and Gaius, lest anyone should say that I had baptized in my own name. Yes, I also baptized the household of Stephanas. Besides, I do not know whether I baptized any other. For Christ did not send me to baptize, but to preach the gospel, not with wisdom of words, lest the cross of Christ should be made of no effect" (1 Cor. 1:10-17).[4]

Who Became for Us Wisdom

"For the message of the cross is foolishness to those who are perishing, but to us who are being saved it is the power of God. For it is written: 'I will destroy the wisdom of the wise, And bring to nothing the understanding of the prudent.' Where is the wise? Where is the scribe? Where is the disputer of this age? Has not God made foolish the wisdom of this world? For since, in the wisdom of God, the world through wisdom did not know God, it pleased God through the foolishness of the message preached to save those who believe. For Jews request a sign, and Greeks seek after wisdom; but we preach Christ crucified, to the Jews a stumbling block and to the Greeks foolishness, but to those who are called, both Jews and Greeks, Christ the power of God and the wisdom of God. Because the foolishness of God is wiser than men, and the weakness of God is stronger than men. For you see your calling, brethren, that not many wise according to the flesh, not many mighty, not many noble, are called. But God has chosen the foolish things of the world to put to shame the wise, and God has chosen the weak things of the world to put to

---

[4] All Scripture quotations, unless otherwise noted, are from the *New King James Version*.

shame the things which are mighty; and the base things of the world and the things which are despised God has chosen, and the things which are not, to bring to nothing the things that are, that no flesh should glory in His presence. But of Him you are in Christ Jesus, who became for us wisdom from God—and righteousness and sanctification and redemption—that, as it is written, 'He who glories, let him glory in the Lord'" (1 Co. 1:18-31).

Not with Persuasive Words of Human Wisdom

"And I, brethren, when I came to you, did not come with excellence of speech or of wisdom declaring to you the testimony of God. For I determined not to know anything among you except Jesus Christ and Him crucified. I was with you in weakness, in fear, and in much trembling. And my speech and my preaching were not with persuasive words of human wisdom, but in demonstration of the Spirit and of power, that your faith should not be in the wisdom of men but in the power of God" (1 Co. 2:1-5).

We Speak the Wisdom of God in a Mystery

"However, we speak wisdom among those who are mature, yet not the wisdom of this age, nor of the rulers of this age, who are coming to nothing. But we speak the wisdom of God in a mystery, the hidden wisdom which God ordained before the ages for our glory, which none of the rulers of this age knew; for had they known, they would not have crucified the Lord of glory. But as it is written: 'Eye has not seen, nor ear heard, nor have entered into the heart of man The things which God has prepared for those who love Him.' But God has revealed them to us through His Spirit. For the Spirit searches all things, yes, the deep things of God. For what man knows the things of a man except the spirit of the man which is in him? Even so no one knows the things of God except the Spirit of God. Now we have received, not the spirit of the world, but the Spirit who is from God, that we might know the things that have been freely given to us by God. These things we also speak, not in words which man's wisdom teaches but which the Holy Spirit teaches, comparing spiritual things with spiritual" (1 Co. 2:6-13).

To Be Wise in This Age

"Let no one deceive himself. If anyone among you seems to be wise in this age, let him become a fool that he may become wise. For the wisdom of this world is foolishness with God. For it is written, 'He catches the wise in their own craftiness'; and again, 'The Lord knows the thoughts of the wise, that they are futile.' Therefore let no one boast in men. For all things are yours: whether Paul or Apollos or Cephas, or the world or life or death, or things present or things to come—all are yours. And you are Christ's, and Christ is God's" (1 Co. 3:18-23).

The Word of Wisdom through the Spirit

"There are diversities of gifts, but the same Spirit. There are differences of ministries, but the same Lord. And there are diversities of activities, but it is the same God who works all in all. But the manifestation of the Spirit is given to each one for the profit of all: for to one is given the word of wisdom through the Spirit, to another the word of knowledge through the same Spirit, to another faith by the same Spirit, to another gifts of healings by the same Spirit, to another the working of miracles, to another prophecy, to another discerning of spirits, to another different kinds of tongues, to another the interpretation of tongues. But one and the same Spirit works all these things, distributing to each one individually as He wills" (1 Co. 12:4-11).

WISDOM IN THE BOOK OF 2 CORINTHIANS

Not with Fleshly Wisdom but by the Grace of God

"For our boasting is this: the testimony of our conscience that we conducted ourselves in the world in simplicity and godly sincerity, not with fleshly wisdom but by the grace of God, and more abundantly toward you. For we are not writing any other things to you than what you read or understand. Now I trust you will understand, even to the end (as also you have understood us in part), that we are your boast as you also are ours, in the day of the Lord Jesus" (2 Co. 1:12-14).

WISDOM IN THE BOOK OF EPHESIANS

To Abound Toward Us in All Wisdom and Prudence

"Blessed be the God and Father of our Lord Jesus Christ, who has blessed us with every spiritual blessing in the heavenly places in Christ, just as He chose us in Him before the foundation of the world, that we should be holy and without blame before Him in love, having predestined us to adoption as sons by Jesus Christ to Himself, according to the good pleasure of His will, to the praise of the glory of His grace, by which He has made us accepted in the Beloved. In Him we have redemption through His blood, the forgiveness of sins, according to the riches of His grace which He made to abound toward us in all wisdom and prudence, having made known to us the mystery of His will, according to His good pleasure which He purposed in Himself, that in the dispensation of the fullness of the times He might gather together in one all things in Christ, both which are in heaven and which are on earth—in Him. In Him also we have obtained an inheritance, being predestined according to the purpose of Him who works all things according to the counsel of His will that we who first trusted in Christ should be to the praise of His glory. In Him you also trusted, after you heard the word of truth, the gospel of your salvation; in whom also, having believed, you were sealed with the Holy Spirit of promise, who is the guarantee of our inheritance until the redemption of the purchased possession, to the praise of His glory" (Eph. 1:3-14).

Give to You the Spirit of Wisdom and Revelation

"Therefore I also, after I heard of your faith in the Lord Jesus and your love for all the saints, do not cease to give thanks for you, making mention of you in my prayers: that the God of our Lord Jesus Christ, the Father of glory, may give to you the spirit of wisdom and revelation in the knowledge of Him, the eyes of your understanding being enlightened; that you may know what is the hope of His calling, what are the riches of the glory of His inheritance in the saints, and what is the exceeding greatness of His power toward us who believe, according to the working of His mighty power which He worked in Christ when He raised Him from the dead and seated Him at His right hand in the heavenly places, far above all principality and power and might and dominion, and every name that is named, not only in this age but also in that which is to come. And He put all things under His feet, and gave Him to be head over all things to the church, which is His body, the fullness of Him who fills all in all" (Eph. 1:15-23).

The Manifold Wisdom of God

"For this reason I, Paul, the prisoner of Christ Jesus for you Gentiles—if indeed you have heard of the dispensation of the grace of God which was given to me for you, how that by revelation He made known to me the mystery (as I have briefly written already, by which, when you read, you may understand my knowledge in the mystery of Christ), which in other ages was not made known to the sons of men, as it has now been revealed by the Spirit to His holy apostles and prophets: that the Gentiles should be fellow heirs, of the same body, and partakers of His promise in Christ through the gospel, of which I became a minister according to the gift of the grace of God given to me by the effective working of His power. To me, who am less than the least of all the saints, this grace was given, that I should preach among the Gentiles the unsearchable riches of Christ, and to make all see what is the fellowship of the mystery, which from the beginning of the ages has been hidden in God who created all things through Jesus Christ; to the intent that now the manifold wisdom of God might be made known by the church to the principalities and powers in the heavenly places, according to the eternal purpose which He accomplished in Christ Jesus our Lord, in whom we have boldness and access with confidence through faith in Him. Therefore I ask that you do not lose heart at my tribulations for you, which is your glory" (Eph. 3:1-13).

WISDOM IN THE BOOK OF COLOSSIANS

In All Wisdom and Spiritual Understanding

"For this reason we also, since the day we heard it, do not cease to pray for you, and to ask that you may be filled with the knowledge of His will in all wisdom and spiritual understanding; that you may walk worthy of the Lord, fully pleasing Him, being fruitful in every good work and increasing in the knowledge of God; strengthened with all might, according to His glorious power, for all patience and longsuffering with joy; giving thanks to the Father who has qualified us to be partakers of the inheritance of the saints in the light. He has delivered us from the power of darkness and conveyed us into the kingdom of the Son of His love, in whom we have redemption through His blood, the forgiveness of sins" (Col. 1:9-14).

Teaching Every Man in All Wisdom

"I now rejoice in my sufferings for you, and fill up in my flesh what is lacking in the afflictions of Christ, for the sake of His body, which is the church, of which I became a minister according to the stewardship from God which was given to me for you, to fulfill the word of God, the mystery which has been hidden from ages and from generations, but now has been revealed to His saints. To them God willed to make known what are the riches of the glory of this mystery among the Gentiles: which is Christ in you, the hope of glory. Him we preach, warning every man and teaching every man in all wisdom, that we may present every man perfect in Christ Jesus. To this end I also labor, striving according to His working which works in me mightily" (Col. 1:24-29).

In Whom Are Hidden All the Treasures of Wisdom

"For I want you to know what a great conflict I have for you and those in Laodicea, and for as many as have not seen my face in the flesh, that their hearts may be encouraged, being knit together in love, and attaining to all riches of the full assurance of understanding, to the knowledge of the mystery of God, both of the Father and of Christ, in whom are hidden all the treasures of wisdom and knowledge. Now this I say lest anyone should deceive you with persuasive words. For though I am absent in the flesh, yet I am with you in spirit, rejoicing to see your good order and the steadfastness of your faith in Christ" (Col. 2:1-5).

An Appearance of Wisdom in Self-imposed Religion

"Therefore, if you died with Christ from the basic principles of the world, why, as though living in the world, do you subject yourselves to regulations—'Do not touch, do not taste, do not handle,' which all concern things which perish with the using—according to the commandments and doctrines of men? These things indeed have an appearance of wisdom in self-imposed religion, false humility, and neglect of the body, but are of no value against the indulgence of the flesh" (Col. 2:20-23).

Dwell in You Richly in all Wisdom

"Therefore, as the elect of God, holy and beloved, put on tender mercies, kindness, humility, meekness, longsuffering; bearing with one another, and forgiving one another, if anyone has a complaint against another; even as Christ forgave you, so you also must do. But above all these things put on love, which is the bond of perfection. And let the peace of God rule in your hearts, to which also you were called in one body; and be thankful. Let the word of Christ dwell in you richly in all wisdom, teaching and admonishing one another in psalms and hymns and spiritual songs, singing with grace in your hearts to the Lord. And whatever you do in word or deed, do all in the name of the Lord Jesus, giving thanks to God the Father through Him" (Col. 3:12-17).

Walk in Wisdom

"Walk in wisdom toward those who are outside, redeeming the time. Let your speech always be with grace, seasoned with salt, that you may know how you ought to answer each one" (Col. 4:5-6).

WISDOM IN THE BOOK OF JAMES

If Any of You Lacks Wisdom, Let Him Ask of God

"If any of you lacks wisdom, let him ask of God, who gives to all liberally and without reproach, and it will be given to him. But let him ask in faith, with no doubting, for he who doubts is like a wave of the sea driven and tossed by the wind. For let not that man suppose that he will receive anything from the Lord; he is a double-minded man, unstable in all his ways" (Jas. 1:5-8).

In the Meekness of Wisdom

"Who is wise and understanding among you? Let him show by good conduct that his works are done in the meekness of wisdom. But if you have bitter envy and self-seeking in your hearts, do not boast and lie against the truth. This wisdom does not descend from above, but is earthly, sensual, demonic. For where envy and self-seeking exist, confusion and every evil thing are there. But the wisdom that is from above is first pure, then peaceable, gentle, willing to yield, full of mercy and good fruits, without partiality and without hypocrisy. Now the fruit of righteousness is sown in peace by those who make peace" (Jas. 3:13-18).

WISDOM IN THE BOOK OF 2 PETER

According to the Wisdom Given to Him

"Therefore, beloved, looking forward to these things, be diligent to be found by Him in peace, without spot and blameless; and consider that the longsuffering of our Lord is salvation—as also our beloved brother Paul, according to the wisdom given to him, has written to you, as also in all his epistles, speaking in them of these things, in which are some things hard to understand, which untaught and unstable people twist to their own destruction, as they do also the rest of the Scriptures. You therefore, beloved, since you know this beforehand, beware lest you also fall from your own steadfastness, being led away with the error of the wicked; but grow in the grace and knowledge of our Lord and Savior Jesus Christ. To Him be the glory both now and forever. Amen" (2 Pe. 3:14-18).

WISDOM IN THE BOOK OF REVELATION

To Receive Power and Riches and Wisdom

"Then I looked, and I heard the voice of many angels around the throne, the living creatures, and the elders; and the number of them was ten thousand times ten thousand, and thousands of thousands, saying with a loud voice: 'Worthy is the Lamb who was slain To receive power and riches and wisdom, And strength and honor and glory and blessing!' And every creature which is in heaven and on the earth and under the earth and such as are in the sea, and all that are in them, I heard saying: 'Blessing and honor and glory and power Be to Him who sits on the throne, And to the Lamb, forever and ever!' Then the four living creatures said, 'Amen!' And the twenty-four elders fell down and worshiped Him who lives forever and ever" (Rev. 5:11-14).

Blessing and Glory and Wisdom and Honor

"After these things I looked, and behold, a great multitude which no one could number, of all nations, tribes, peoples, and tongues, standing before the throne and before the Lamb, clothed with white robes, with palm branches in their hands, and crying out with a loud voice, saying, 'Salvation belongs to our God who sits on the throne, and to the Lamb!' All the angels stood around the throne and the elders and the four living creatures, and fell on their faces before the throne and worshiped God, saying: 'Amen! Blessing and glory and wisdom, thanksgiving and honor and power and might, be to our God forever and ever. Amen'" (Rev. 7:9-12).

Here Is Wisdom

"Then I saw another beast coming up out of the earth, and he had two horns like a lamb and spoke like a dragon. And he exercises all the authority of the first beast in his presence, and causes the earth and those who dwell in it to worship the first beast, whose deadly wound was healed. He performs great signs, so that he even makes fire come down from heaven on the earth in the sight of men. And he deceives those who dwell on the earth by those signs which he was granted to do in the sight of the beast, telling those who dwell on the earth to make an image to the beast who was wounded by the sword and lived. He was granted power to give breath to the image of the beast, that the image of the beast should both speak and cause as many as would not worship the image of the beast to be killed. He causes all, both small and great, rich and poor, free and slave, to receive a mark on their right hand or on their foreheads, and that no one may buy or sell except one who has the mark or the name of the beast, or the number of his name. Here is wisdom. Let him who has understanding calculate the number of the beast, for it is the number of a man: His number is 666" (Rev. 13:11-18).

Here Is the Mind Which Has Wisdom

"The beast that you saw was, and is not, and will ascend out of the bottomless pit and go to perdition. And those who dwell on the earth will marvel, whose names are not written in the Book of Life from the foundation of the world, when they see the beast that was, and is not, and yet is. Here is the mind which has wisdom: The seven heads are seven mountains on which the woman sits. There are also seven kings. Five have fallen, one is, and the other has not yet come. And when he comes, he must continue a short time. And the beast that was, and is not, is himself also the eighth, and is of the seven, and is going to perdition. The ten horns which you saw are ten kings who have received no kingdom as yet, but they receive authority for one hour as kings with the beast. These are of one mind, and they will give their power and authority to the beast. These will make war with the Lamb, and the Lamb will overcome them, for He is Lord of lords and King of kings; and those who are with Him are called, chosen, and faithful" (Rev. 17:8-14).

REVELATION IN THE NEW TESTAMENT

IN THE BOOK OF LUKE

A Light of Revelation

"And there was a man in Jerusalem whose name was Simeon; and this man was righteous and devout, looking for the consolation of Israel; and the Holy Spirit was upon him. And it had been revealed to him by the Holy Spirit that he would not see death before he had seen the Lord's Christ. And he came in the Spirit into the temple; and when the parents brought in the child Jesus, to carry out for Him the custom of the Law, then he took Him into his arms, and blessed God, and said, 'Now Lord, You are releasing Your bond-servant to depart in peace, According to Your word; for my eyes have seen Your salvation, which You have prepared in the presence of all peoples, A LIGHT OF REVELATION TO THE GENTILES, And the glory of Your people Israel" (Lu. 2:25-32).

IN THE BOOK OF ROMANS

Revelation of the Righteous Judgment of God

"Therefore you have no excuse, everyone of you who passes judgment, for in that which you judge another, you condemn yourself; for you who judge practice the same things. And we know that the judgment of God rightly falls upon those who practice such things. But do you suppose this, O man, when you pass judgment on those who practice such things and do the same yourself, that you will escape the judgment of God? Or do you think lightly of the riches of His kindness and tolerance and patience, not knowing that the kindness of God leads you to repentance? But because of your stubbornness and unrepentant heart you are storing up wrath for yourself in the day of wrath and revelation of the righteous judgment of God, who WILL RENDER TO EACH PERSON ACCORDING TO HIS DEEDS: to those who by perseverance in doing good seek for glory and honor and immortality, eternal life; but to those who are selfishly ambitious and do not obey the truth, but obey unrighteousness, wrath and indignation. There will be tribulation and distress for every soul of man who does evil, of the Jew first and also of the Greek, but glory and honor and peace to everyone who does good, to the Jew first and also to the Greek. For there is no partiality with God" (Ro. 2:1-11).

According To the Revelation of the Mystery

"Now to Him who is able to establish you according to my gospel and the preaching of Jesus Christ, according to the revelation of the mystery which has been kept secret for long ages past, but now is manifested, and by the Scriptures of the prophets, according to the commandment of the eternal God, has been made known to all the nations, leading to obedience of faith; to the only wise God, through Jesus Christ, be the glory forever. Amen" (Ro. 16:25-27).

IN THE BOOK OF 1 CORINTHIANS

Awaiting Eagerly the Revelation of our Lord Jesus Christ

"I thank my God always concerning you for the grace of God which was given you in Christ Jesus, that in everything you were enriched in Him, in all speech and all knowledge, even as the testimony concerning Christ was confirmed in you, so that you are not lacking in any gift, awaiting eagerly the revelation of our Lord Jesus Christ, who will also confirm you to the end, blameless in the day of our Lord Jesus Christ. God is faithful, through whom you were called into fellowship with His Son, Jesus Christ our Lord" (1Co. 1:4-9).

By Way of Revelation or of Knowledge or of Prophecy or of Teaching

"But now, brethren, if I come to you speaking in tongues, what will I profit you unless I speak to you either by way of revelation or of knowledge or of prophecy or of teaching? Yet even lifeless things, either flute or harp, in producing a sound, if they do not produce a distinction in the tones, how will it be known what is played on the flute or on the harp? For if the bugle produces an indistinct sound, who will prepare himself for battle? So also you, unless you utter by the tongue speech that is clear, how will it be known what is spoken? For you will be speaking into the air. There are, perhaps, a great many kinds of languages in the world, and no kind is without meaning. If then I do not know the meaning of the language, I will be to the one who speaks a barbarian, and the one who speaks will be a barbarian to me. So also you, since you are zealous of spiritual gifts, seek to abound for the edification of the church" (1Co. 14:6-12).

Has a Revelation

"What is the outcome then, brethren? When you assemble, each one has a psalm, has a teaching, has a revelation, has a tongue, has an interpretation. Let all things be done for edification. If anyone speaks in a tongue, it should be by two or at the most three, and each in turn, and one must interpret; but if there is no interpreter, he must keep silent in the church; and let him speak to himself and to God. Let two or three prophets speak, and let the others pass judgment. But if a revelation is made to another who is seated, the first one must keep silent. For you can all prophesy one by one, so that all may learn and all may be exhorted; and the spirits of prophets are subject to prophets; for God is not a God of confusion but of peace, as in all the churches of the saints" (1Co. 14:26-33).

IN THE BOOK OF GALATIANS

I Received it through a Revelation of Jesus Christ

"For I would have you know, brethren, that the gospel which was preached by me is not according to man. For I neither received it from man, nor was I taught it, but I received it through a revelation of Jesus Christ" (Ga. 1:11-12).

Because of a Revelation

"Then after an interval of fourteen years I went up again to Jerusalem with Barnabas, taking Titus along also. It was because of a revelation that I went up; and I submitted to them the gospel which I preach among the Gentiles, but I did so in private to those who were of reputation, for fear that I might be running, or had run, in vain. But not even Titus, who was with me, though he was a Greek, was compelled to be circumcised. But it was because of the false brethren secretly brought in, who had sneaked in to spy out our liberty which we have in Christ Jesus, in order to bring us into bondage. But we did not yield in subjection to them for even an hour, so that the truth of the gospel would remain with you. But from those who were of high reputation (what they were makes no difference to me; God shows no partiality) — well, those who were of reputation contributed nothing to me. But on the contrary, seeing that I had been entrusted with the gospel to the uncircumcised, just as Peter had been to the circumcised (for He who effectually worked for Peter in his apostleship to the circumcised effectually worked for me also to the Gentiles), and recognizing the grace that had been given to me, James and Cephas and John, who were reputed to be pillars, gave to me and Barnabas the right hand of fellowship, so that we might go to the Gentiles and they to the circumcised. They only asked us to remember the poor — the very thing I also was eager to do" (Ga. 2:1-10).

IN THE BOOK OF EPHESIANS

A Spirit of Wisdom and of Revelation in the Knowledge of Him

"For this reason I too, having heard of the faith in the Lord Jesus which exists among you and your love for all the saints, do not cease giving thanks for you, while making mention of you in my prayers; that the God of our Lord Jesus Christ, the Father of glory, may give to you a spirit of wisdom and of revelation in the knowledge of Him. I pray that the eyes of your heart may be enlightened, so that you will know what is the hope of His calling, what are the riches of the glory of His inheritance in the saints, and what is the surpassing greatness of His power toward us who believe. These are in accordance with the working of the strength of His might which He brought about in Christ, when He raised Him from the dead and seated Him at His right hand in the heavenly places, far above all rule and authority and power and dominion, and every name that is named, not only in this age but also in the one to come. And He put all things in subjection under His feet, and gave Him as head over all things to the church, which is His body, the fullness of Him who fills all in all" (Eph. 1:15-23).

By Revelation There Was Made Known to Me the Mystery

"For this reason I, Paul, the prisoner of Christ Jesus for the sake of you Gentiles — if indeed you have heard of the stewardship of God's grace which was given to me for you; that by revelation there was made known to me the mystery, as I wrote before in brief. By referring to this, when you read you can understand my insight into the mystery of Christ, which in other generations was not made known to the sons of men, as it has now been revealed to His holy apostles and prophets in the Spirit; to be specific, that the Gentiles are fellow heirs and fellow members of the body, and fellow partakers of the promise in Christ Jesus through the gospel, of which I was made a minister, according to the gift of God's grace which was given to me according to the working of His power. To me, the very least of all saints, this grace was given, to preach to the Gentiles the unfathomable riches of Christ, and to bring to light what is the administration of the mystery which for ages has been hidden in God who created all things; so that the manifold wisdom of God might now be made known through the church to the rulers and the authorities in the heavenly places. This was in accordance with the eternal purpose which He carried out in Christ Jesus our Lord, in whom we have boldness and confident access through faith in Him. Therefore I ask you not to lose heart at my tribulations on your behalf, for they are your glory" (Eph. 3:1-13).

IN THE BOOK OF 1 PETER

Glory and Honor at the Revelation of Jesus Christ

"Blessed be the God and Father of our Lord Jesus Christ, who according to His great mercy has caused us to be born again to a living hope through the resurrection of Jesus Christ from the dead, to obtain an inheritance which is imperishable and undefiled and will not fade away, reserved in heaven for you, who are protected by the power of God through faith for a salvation ready to be revealed in the last time. In this you greatly rejoice, even though now for a little while, if necessary, you have been distressed by various trials, so that the proof of your faith, being more precious than gold which is perishable, even though tested by fire, may be found to result in praise and glory and honor at the revelation of Jesus Christ; and though you have not seen Him, you love Him, and though you do not see Him now, but believe in Him, you greatly rejoice with joy inexpressible and full of glory, obtaining as the outcome of your faith the salvation of your souls" (1Pe. 1:3-9).

Brought to You at the Revelation

"Therefore, prepare your minds for action, keep sober in spirit, fix your hope completely on the grace to be brought to you at the revelation of Jesus Christ. As obedient children, do not be conformed to the former lusts which were yours in your ignorance, but like the Holy One who called you, be holy yourselves also in all your behavior; because it is written, ''YOU SHALL BE HOLY, FOR I AM HOLY" (1Pe. 1:13-16).

The Revelation of His Glory

"Beloved, do not be surprised at the fiery ordeal among you, which comes upon you for your testing, as though some strange thing were happening to you; but to the degree that you share the sufferings of Christ, keep on rejoicing, so that also at the revelation of His glory you may rejoice with exultation. If you are reviled for the name of Christ, you are blessed, because the Spirit of glory and of God rests on you. Make sure that none of you suffers as a murderer, or thief, or evildoer, or a troublesome meddler; but if anyone suffers as a Christian, he is not to be ashamed, but is to glorify God in this name. For it is time for judgment to begin with the household of God; and if it begins with us first, what will be the outcome for those who do not obey the gospel of God? AND IF IT IS WITH DIFFICULTY THAT THE RIGHTEOUS IS SAVED, WHAT WILL BECOME OF THE GODLESS MAN AND THE SINNER? Therefore, those also who suffer according to the will of God shall entrust their souls to a faithful Creator in doing what is right" (1Pe. 4:12-19).

IN THE BOOK OF REVELATION

The Revelation of Jesus Christ

"The Revelation of Jesus Christ, which God gave Him to show to His bond-servants, the things which must soon take place; and He sent and communicated it by His angel to His bond-servant John, who testified to the word of God and to the testimony of Jesus Christ, even to all that he saw. Blessed is he who reads and those who hear the words of the prophecy, and heed the things which are written in it; for the time is near" (Re. 1:1-3).

DAILY FAITH CONFESSIONS

(These are not direct quotations from the Bible but
are paraphrased confessions based on scripture.)
SAY THEM OUT LOUD.

I am God's child (Jn. 1:12). I am royalty (1 Pet.
2:9). I am hidden with Christ in God (Col. 3:3). I am
united with the Lord (1 Cor. 6:17). I am a friend of
Christ (Jn. 15:15). I am raised up with Him, and
seated with Him in heavenly places in Christ Jesus
(Eph. 2:6). I was bought with a price (1 Cor. 6:19-20).
I am blessed when I come in, and blessed shall I be
when I go out (Deut. 28:6). I am a personal witness
of Christ (Acts 1:8). I am a saint who prays in the
Holy Spirit to keep myself in the love of God (Jude
1:20-21). I draw near with confidence to the throne of
grace (Heb. 4:16). I have been adopted by the Father
(Eph. 1:5). I am the salt and light of the earth (Mt.
5:13). I am the head and not the tail, and I am above,
and not underneath. I am the lender and not the
borrower (Deut. 28:13). I have authority to trample
serpents and scorpions and over all the power of the
enemy (Lk. 10:19). I am a member of the body of
Christ (1 Cor. 12:27). God blessed me to be fruitful,
and multiply, and replenish the earth, and subdue it:
and have dominion (Gen. 1:28). I cannot be
separated from God's love (Ro. 8:39). The good work
God has begun in me will be perfected (Phil. 1:5). I
can do all things through Christ who strengthens me
(Phil. 4:13). No weapon that is formed against me
will prosper (Is. 54:17). So then faith cometh by
hearing, and hearing by the word of God (Ro. 10:17
KJV). Faith is my currency to operate in the kingdom

of God (Ro. 14:23). I am God's workmanship created in Christ Jesus for good works, which God prepared beforehand (Eph. 2:10). I have been appointed to bear fruit, and that my fruit would remain (Jn. 15:16). I am being wise when I am winning souls for King Jesus (Pr. 11:30). My body is the temple of the Holy Spirit (1 Cor. 6:19). I have access to God through the Holy Spirit (Eph. 2:18). I have been justified (Ro. 5:1). Therefore there is now no condemnation for those who are in Christ Jesus (Ro. 8:1). Greater is He who is in me than he who is in the world (1 Jn. 4:4). I will do greater works than Jesus because He went to the Father (Jn. 14:12). As God was with Moses, He will be with me; God will not fail me or forsake me (Jos. 1:5). I see myself the way God see me. God sees me as a king (Gen, 17:6, Rev. 1:6) God sees me as royalty (1 Pet. 2:9). God sees me as the righteousness of God in Christ, bold as a lion (Ro. 3:22, Pr. 28:1). God sees me without spot or wrinkle because of the blood of Jesus (1 Pet. 1:19). I am having faith for big things because God owns everything and I'm His son (Ps. 24:1). No man will be able to stand before me all the days of my life (Jos. 1:5). My Father is glorified by this that I bear much fruit, and proves I'm a disciple (see Jn. 15:8). I think big and confess big things because God is big (Ps. 24:1). I will respect God for the big God that He is and my mouth will create whatever I want (Lk. 6:45). I no longer think of millions, my renewed mind thinks of billions because the wealth of the wicked is laid up for the righteous (Pr. 13:22). The sinner's job is to gather and collect for the one who is good in God's sight (Ecc. 2:26). Redemption is not complete without prosperity. Jesus hung on the cross so I can have the whole package, not just salvation (2 Cor. 8:9). I don't have to qualify, Jesus has qualified me. Jesus reversed the curse. The devil is a liar, and Jesus is the Messiah. Jesus is made unto me wisdom, righteousness, sanctification, and redemption (1 Cor. 1:30). I submit to God, I resist the devil and he flees from me (Jas. 4:7). For God has not given me the spirit of fear; but of power, and of love, and of a sound mind (2 Tim. 1:7). The Holy Spirit will teach me all things (Jn. 14:26). The Holy Spirit will guide me into all truth (Jn.16:13). The Holy Spirit abides in me, and I don't need anyone to teach me, but the anointing teaches me all things (1 Jn. 2:27). I quench fiery darts from the wicked one with the shield of faith (Eph. 6:16). I stand firm against the schemes of the devil (Eph. 6:11). I already have the victory and Satan cannot back me up. I advance and hold. Advance and hold to victory after victory (2 Cor. 2:14). I walk in love and live by faith (Gal. 5:6). I have been redeemed from the curse of the law, poverty, sickness, and spiritual death (Gal. 3:13; Deut. 28). I bear much fruit. I'm God's workmanship created beforehand for good works (Eph. 2:10). God's favor is on my life (Ps. 3:8). God blesses me and His favor surrounds me as with a shield (Ps. 5:12). The kingdom of God is within me (Lk. 17:21). I have a production plant inside of me that bears fruit to change the world (Gen. 1:28). God gives me power to get wealth to establish His covenant on earth (Deut. 8:18). I am blessed to be a blessing (Gen. 12:2). I have Satan on the run and will make a mockery of him (Jas. 4:7). No man will be able to stand before me all the days of my life (Jos. 1:5). God's angels keep me in all my ways (Ps. 91:11).

PRAYER FOR SALVATION

Say the following prayer out loud.

Heavenly Father, I am a sinner and I need a Savior. I confess Jesus Christ as the Lord of my life. I repent of all my sins. Father, I truly believe you raised Jesus from the dead. I pray this prayer in Jesus' name. Father, I am your child because Jesus is my Lord. I want to receive the fullness of the Holy Spirit. Holy Spirit come into me and fill me so I can be a mighty witness for King Jesus. I pray this prayer in Jesus' name. Amen.

PRAYER FOR BAPTISM OF THE HOLY SPIRIT

Say the following prayer out loud.

Father, I am your child because Jesus is my Lord. Jesus said, "How much more shall your heavenly Father give the Holy Spirit to those who ask Him." I ask you now in the name of Jesus to fill me with the Holy Spirit. Thank you, Father, I received the baptism of the Holy Spirit by faith. I yield my vocal organs and expect to speak in tongues as the Holy Spirit gives me utterance in Jesus name. Father, I plan to pray in the Holy Spirit building myself up on my most holy faith, and keep myself in the love of God, as mentioned in Jude 20 and 21. In Jesus name I decree it. Amen.

ABOUT THE AUTHOR

Eugene Carvalho is an evangelist, an administrator, an intercessor, and Christian author of two hundred twenty-four books. He is the founder of Receiving by Faith and evangelizes through his Christian literature. He holds a bachelor's degree in biblical studies and a double minor in pastoral ministry and world missions. He also holds a master's degree in practical theology. Eugene prayed for a translator and God sent his wife Mercedes who has a six-year degree in Spanish from a university in Tampico, Mexico. They have participated in evangelism in the streets of Mexico for many years. They have also traveled to churches all over the United States and the nation of Mexico winning souls and preaching the gospel of the kingdom. Their ministry website is: www.receivingbyfaith.org.

BOOKS BY EUGENE IN ENGLISH

For a <u>complete list</u> of other books by Eugene visit receivingbyfaith.org or amazon.com.

Receiving by Faith
Faith for Every Day: 365 Daily Devotions
Faith Cometh by Hearing, and Hearing by the Word of God
Faith, Hope, and Love
Walk in Love and Live by Faith
Topical Christian Handbook and Scripture Guide
The Gospel Is the Power of God unto Salvation
Seed Time and Harvest Time
Your New Identity in Christ
The Cross and the Blood
The Holy Spirit
The Attributes of God
The Favor of God
The Glory of God
The Grace of God
The Love of God
The Power of God
The Promises of God
The Spirit of God
The Throne of God
The Virtues of God
The New Testament Church: A Survey from the Book of Ephesians
Vengeance and Recompense
God's Angel's
Prayer and Fasting

Old Testament Miracles
New Testament Miracles
God's Mighty Prophets
A Survey of Jesus Through the Epistles
The Fear of the Lord Is the Beginning of
Knowledge; Fools Despise Wisdom and
Instruction
The Psalms of David
Faith Without Works Is Dead
The Names of Jesus
Mountain Moving Confessions
In Him Was Life; and the Life Was the Light of
Men
Visions and Dreams
Having Shod Your Feet with the Preparation of
the Gospel of Peace
Blessed Beyond Measure
The Righteous Will Flourish like The Palm Tree
Christ Heals: What the Bible Has to Say
Jesus Is the Way, and the Truth, and the Life
My Peace I Give to You
Balancing Grace and Truth
The Old and New Testament Supernatural Acts of
God Almighty
Praise and Worship Changes Everything
Understanding the Importance of Authority
If You Are Willing and Obedient
Have Faith in Jesus and the Finished Work of the
Cross
Have Life More Abundantly
Pray in the Holy Spirit; Guard and Keep
Yourselves in the Love of God

Spiritual Formation: Unleashing the Kingdom of God within You

You Have Authority and Power: Take Back What the Devil Stole

Be Strong and Courageous

Prayer and Praise: The Big Artillery

Apostles and Prophets: The Foundation of the Church

Covenant: What the Bible Has to Say

Sow Then Reap a Harvest

God Has Not Given Us a Spirit of Timidity, But of Power, Love, and Discipline

Blessed and Highly Favored

Grace and Peace Be Multiplied Unto You

Your Word Is a Lamp to Me Feet

John: A Key Word Study Made Simple

For Momentary, Light Affliction Is Producing For Us an Eternal Weight of Glory

Prayer Is Powerful: What the Bible Has to Say

My People Are Destroyed By Lack of Knowledge

God Deserves Pure Worship

The Mouth of the Righteous is a Fountain of Life

The Lord Requires Integrity

Weeping May Last for the Night, But a Shout of Joy Comes in the Morning

A Topical Look at the Book of Deuteronomy

A Topical Look at the Book of Psalms

A Topical Look at the Book of Proverbs

A Topical Look at the Book of Isaiah

A Topical Look at the Book of John

A Topical Look at the Book of Hebrews

A Topical Look at the Book of Revelation

BOOKS BY EUGENE IN SPANISH

Las Promesas de Dios
Los Salmos de David
Lo Sobrenatural: Lo que la Bíblia Tiene que Decir
Una Mirada Topica Del Libro De Los Salmos
Dios es Amor: Lo que la Biblia Tiene que Decir
La Adquisición de la Sabiduría es Vital: Lo que la
Biblia Tiene que Decir

NOTES